W9-ALM-801

I Like to Visit

The Library

Jacqueline Laks Gorman

**Reading consultant: Susan Nations, M.Ed.,
author/literacy coach/consultant**

Please visit our web site at: www.earlyliteracy.cc
For a free color catalog describing Weekly Reader® Early Learning Library's list
of high-quality books, call 1-877-445-5824 (USA) or 1-800-387-3178 (Canada).
Weekly Reader® Early Learning Library's fax: (414) 336-0164.

Library of Congress Cataloging-in-Publication Data

Gorman, Jacqueline Laks, 1955–
    The library / Jacqueline Laks Gorman.
        p. cm. — (I like to visit)
    Includes bibliographical references and index.
    ISBN 0-8368-4452-1 (lib. bdg.)
    ISBN 0-8368-4459-9 (softcover)
    1. Libraries—Juvenile literature. I. Title. II. Series.
    Z665.5G67   2005
    027—dc22   2004057229

This edition first published in 2005 by
Weekly Reader® Early Learning Library
330 West Olive Street, Suite 100
Milwaukee, WI 53212 USA

Copyright © 2005 by Weekly Reader® Early Learning Library

Art direction: Tammy West
Editor: JoAnn Early Macken
Cover design and page layout: Kami Koenig
Picture research: Diane Laska-Swanke

Picture credits: Cover, pp. 5, 7, 9, 11, 13, 15, 17, 19, 21 Gregg Andersen

Printed in the United States of America

1 2 3 4 5 6 7 8 9 09 08 07 06 05

Note to Educators and Parents

Reading is such an exciting adventure for young children! They are beginning to integrate their oral language skills with written language. To encourage children along the path to early literacy, books must be colorful, engaging, and interesting; they should invite the young reader to explore both the print and the pictures.

I Like to Visit is a new series designed to help children read about familiar and exciting places. Each book explores a different place that kids like to visit and describes what a visitor can see and do there.

Each book is specially designed to support the young reader in the reading process. The familiar topics are appealing to young children and invite them to read — and re-read — again and again. The full-color photographs and enhanced text further support the student during the reading process.

In addition to serving as wonderful picture books in schools, libraries, homes, and other places where children learn to love reading, these books are specifically intended to be read within an instructional guided reading group. This small group setting allows beginning readers to work with a fluent adult model as they make meaning from the text. After children develop fluency with the text and content, the book can be read independently. Children and adults alike will find these books supportive, engaging, and fun!

— Susan Nations, M.Ed., author, literacy coach,
and consultant in literacy development

I like to visit the library. The library is full of books. I like to look at books in the library.

I like to look at
books for children.
I know where to find
them. They are
near the aquarium.

Some books tell stories. Some books have pictures. Some books are about real true things. Which books do you like?

9

I am looking for a book. I want to read about dogs. The librarian can help me find the book I want.

The librarian reads
stories to children.
I like to hear stories.
Do you like to hear
stories, too?

I like to read in the library. I like to read books and magazines. This book is about pets.

I am quiet in the library. Other people like to read, too! They need quiet to read.

I like to use the computer. It helps me learn. I play games on the computer, too.

I have my own library card. I use it to borrow books. I always bring them back on time!

21

Glossary

borrow — to take something that belongs to someone else, with permission, and promise to return it

librarian — a person who works in a library

library — a place where people can use or borrow books, magazines, videos, and other things

library card — a special card that can be used to borrow things from a library

quiet — not loud or noisy

For More Information

Books

A Day with a Librarian. Hard Work (series). Jan Kottke (Children's Press).

Going to the Library. First Time (series). Melinda Beth Radabaugh (Heinemann Library).

Let's Visit the Library. Our Community (series). Marianne Johnston (PowerKids Press).

Librarian. People in My Community (series). Jacqueline Laks Gorman (Weekly Reader Early Learning Library)

Web Sites

Seminole County Public Library System Kids' Page
www.scpl.lib.fl.us/kids/
Book reviews, stories, and links to author Web sites

Index

About the Author

Jacqueline Laks Gorman is a writer and editor. She grew up in New York City and began her career working on encyclopedias and other reference books. Since then, she has worked on many different kinds of books and written several children's books. She lives with her husband, David, and children, Colin and Caitlin, in DeKalb, Illinois. They all like to visit many kinds of places.